My Family

by Jean Thomas

Photographed by Ray Boudreau

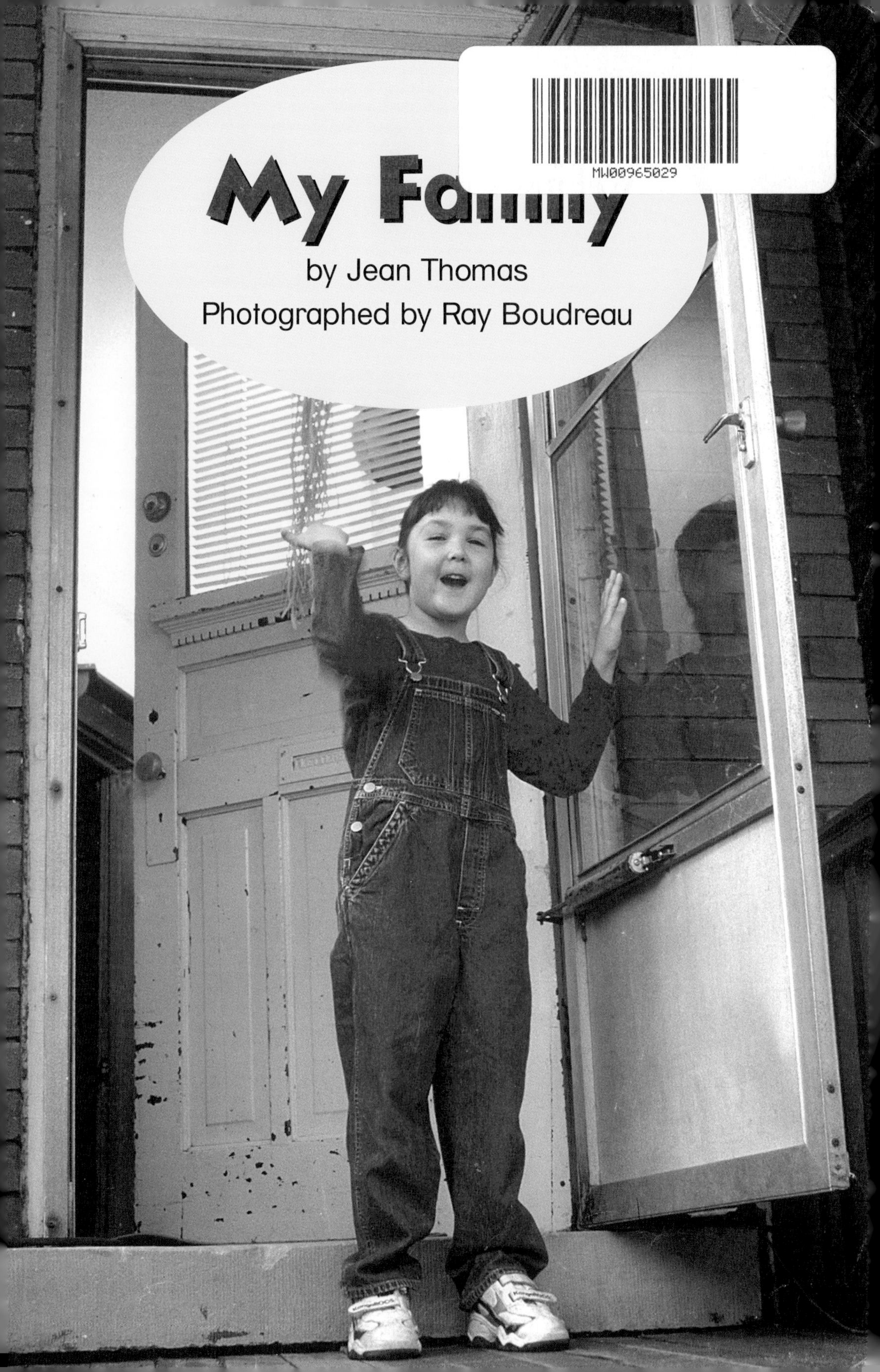

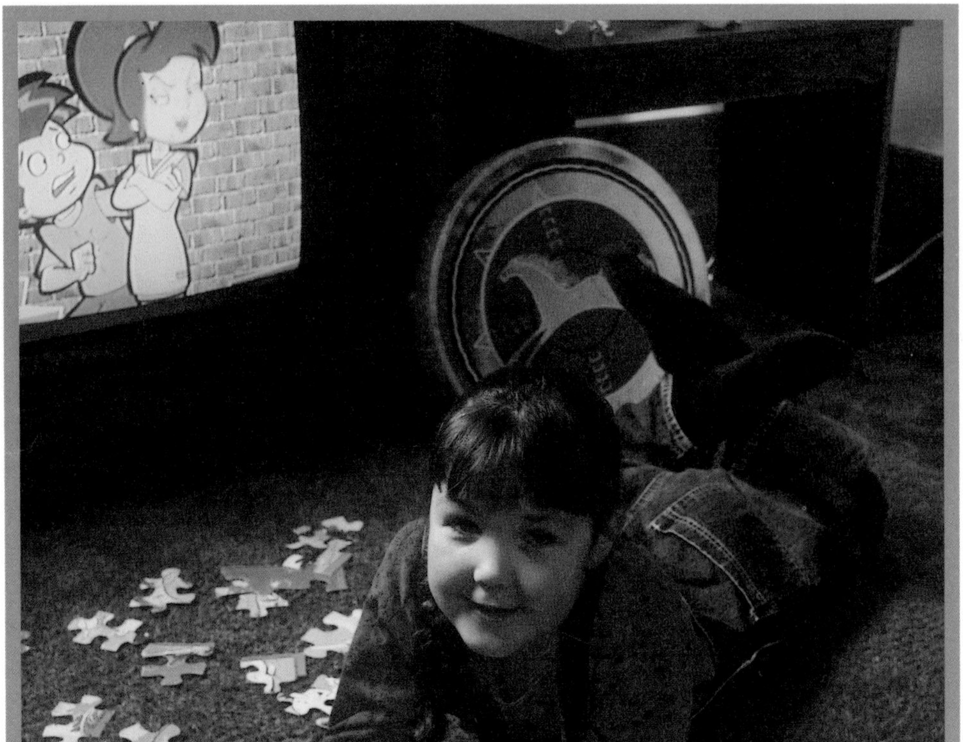

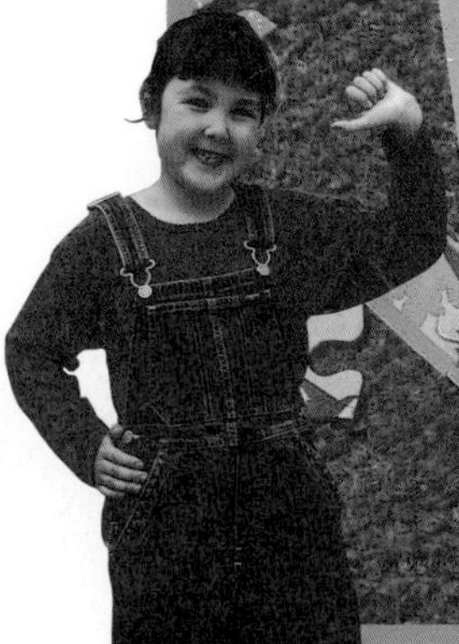

me

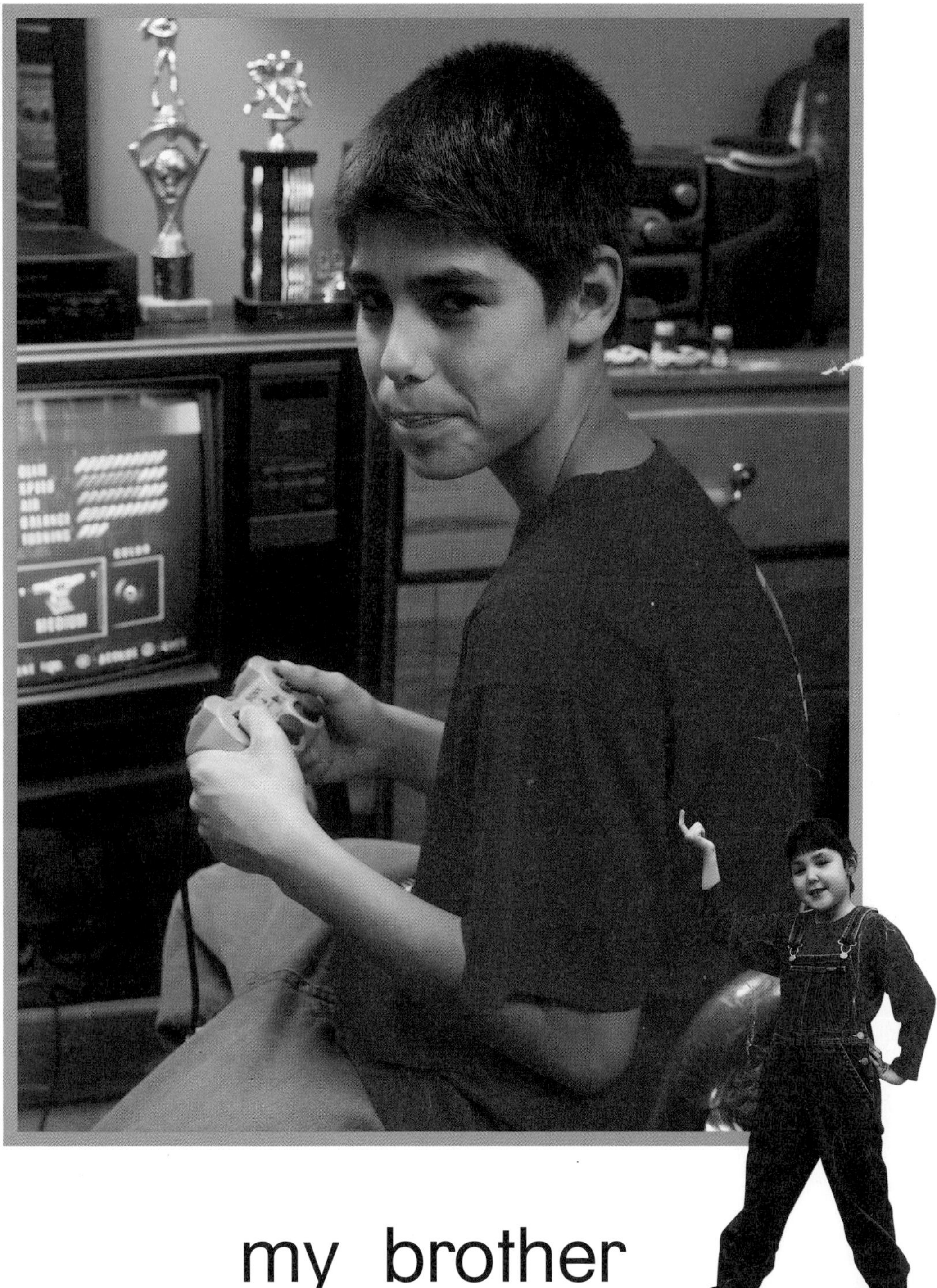

my brother

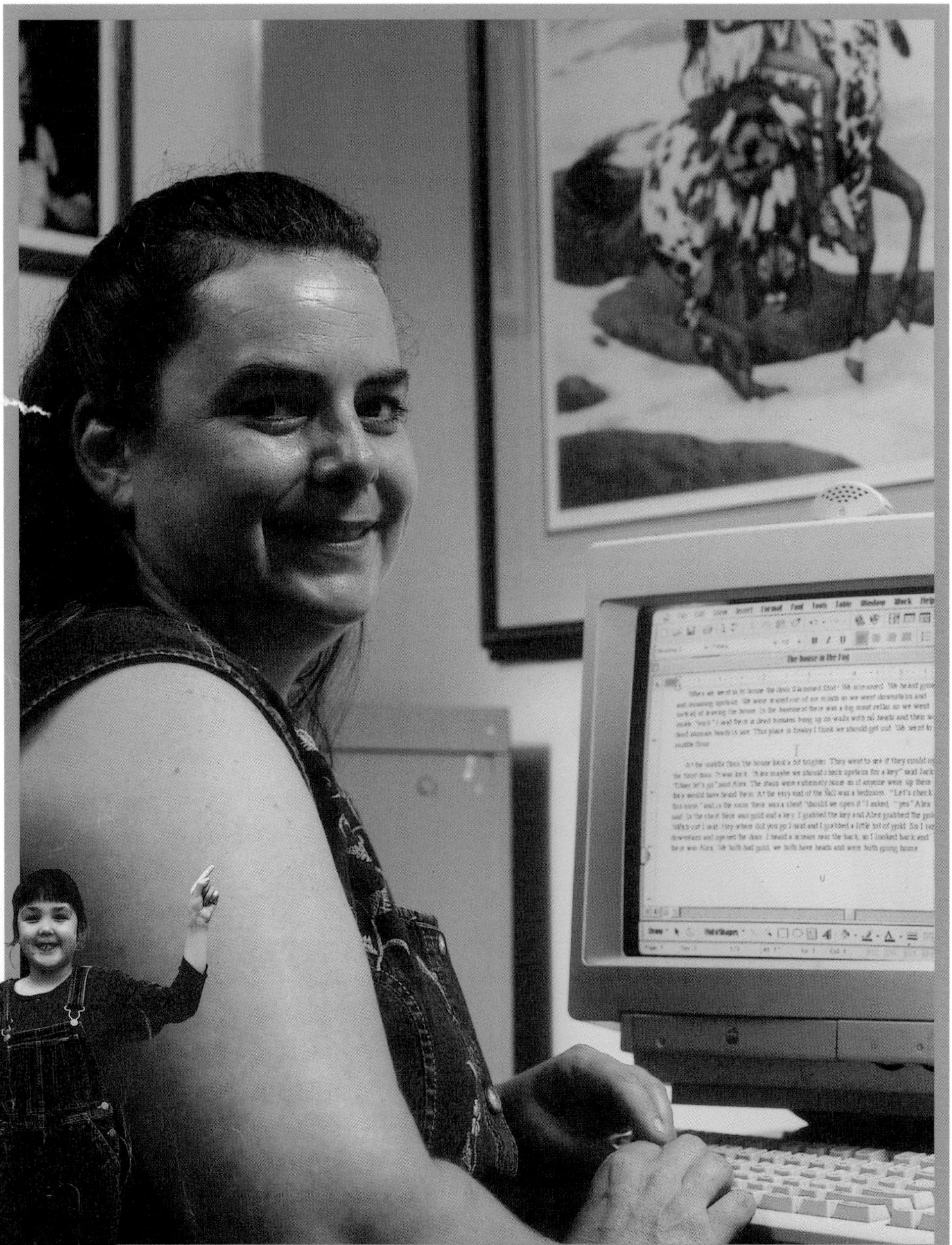

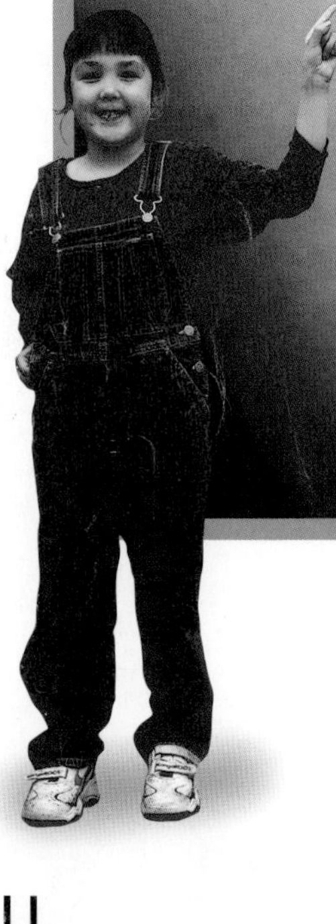

my mom

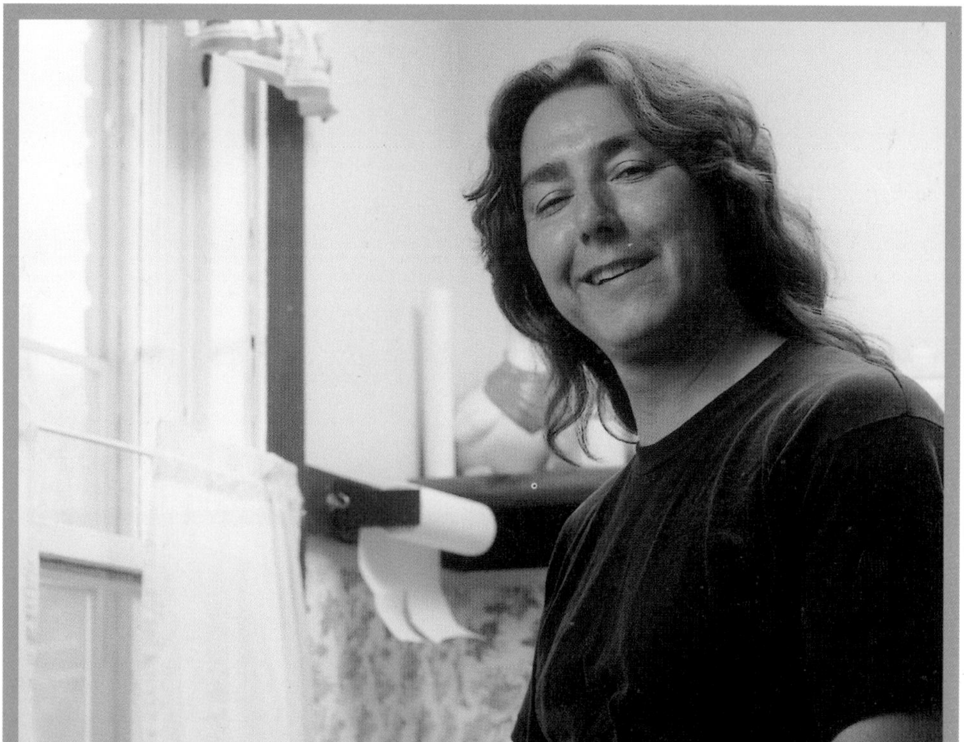

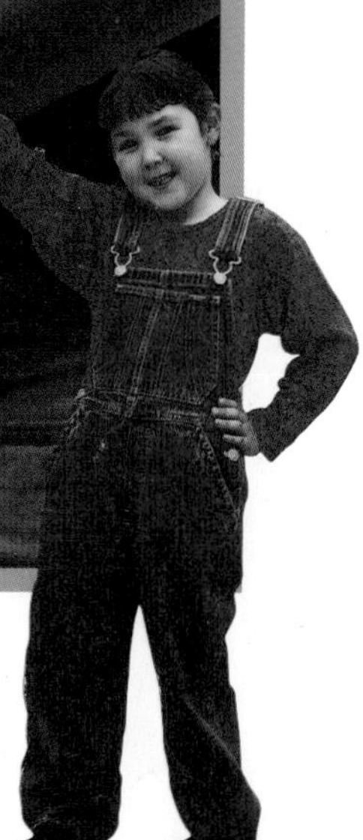

my dad

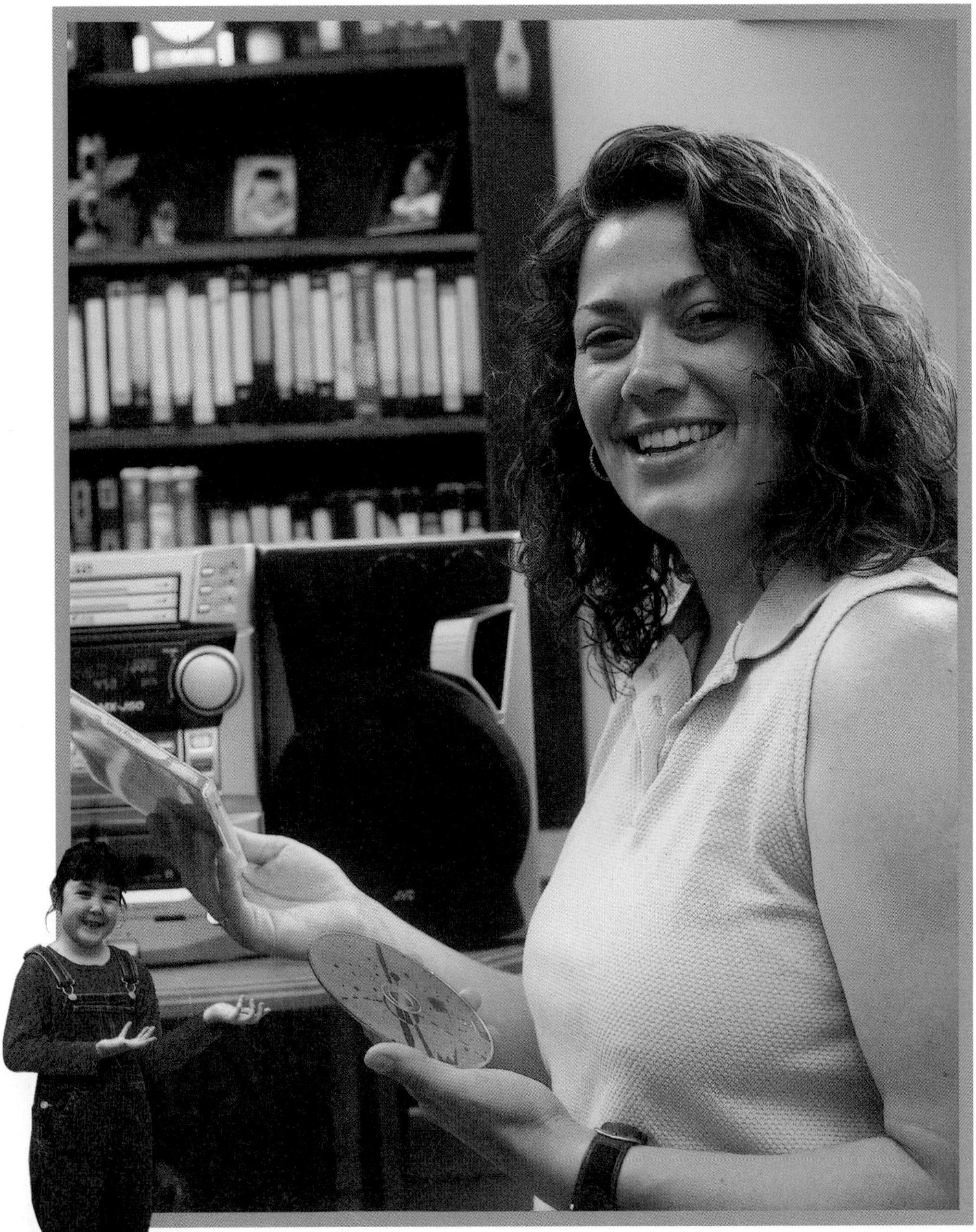

my aunt

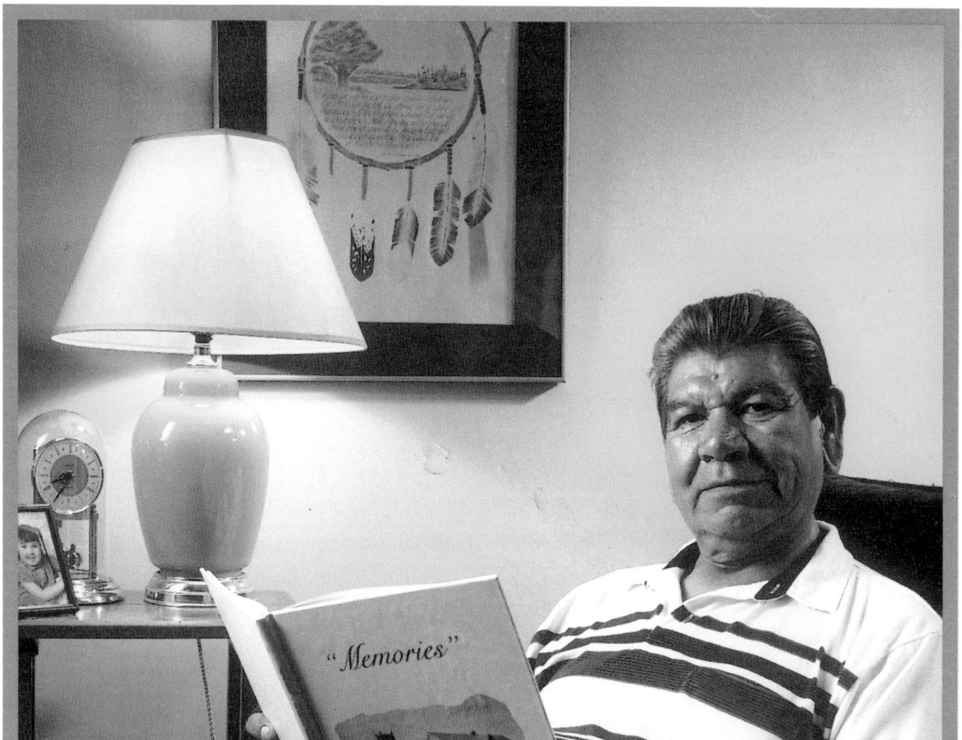

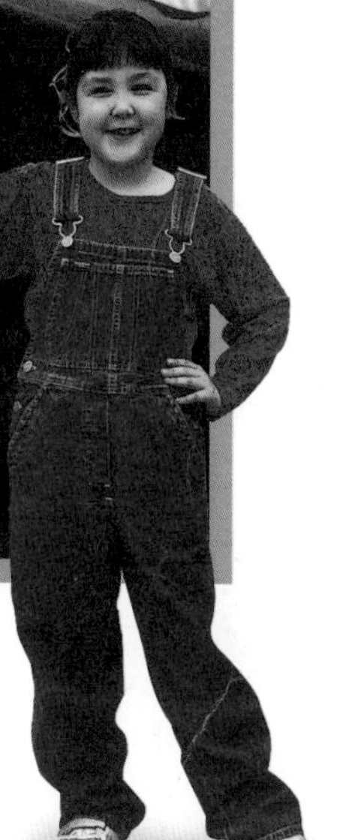

my grandpa

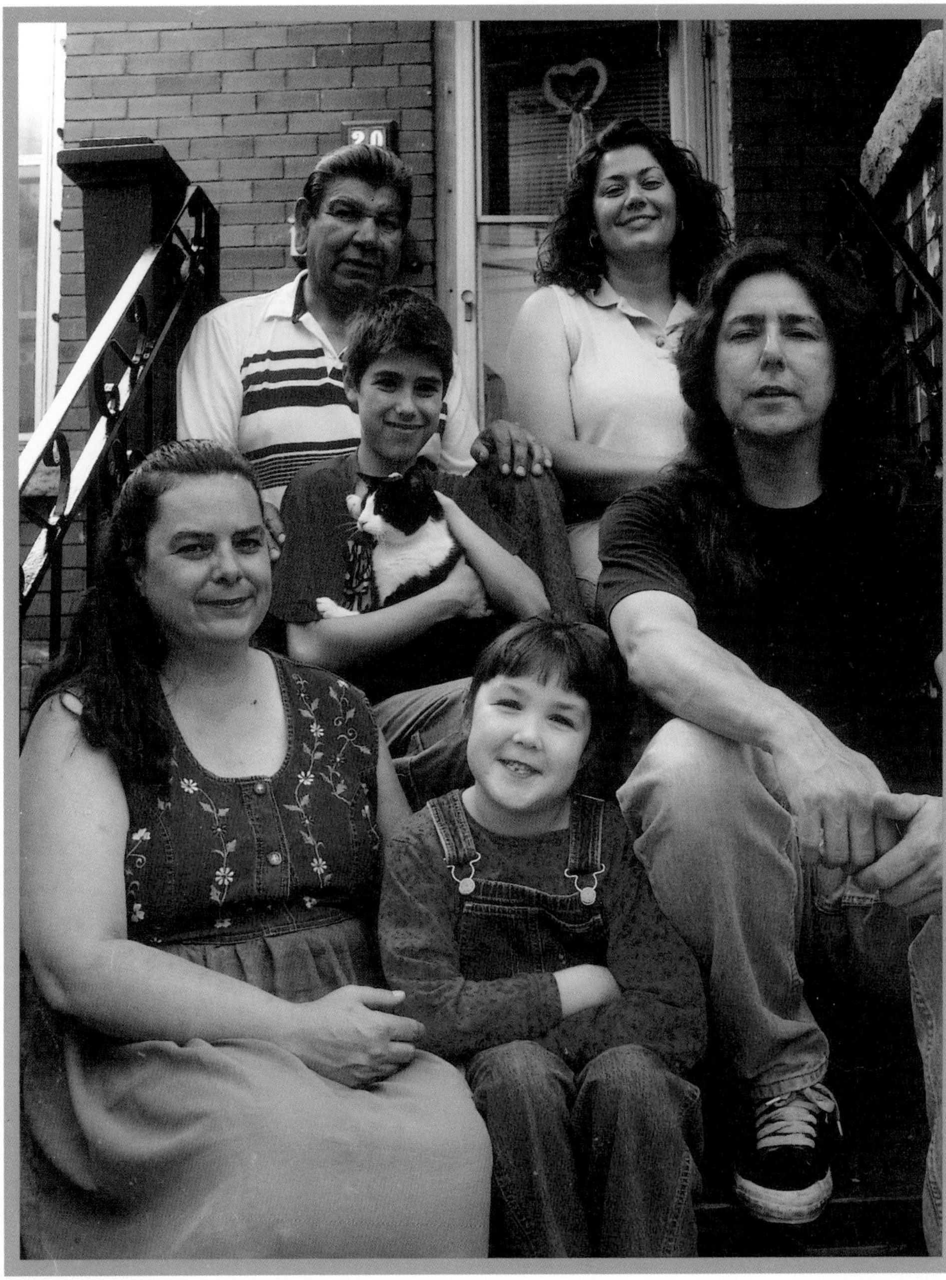

my family